Design of the Times:

How to Plan Glorious Landscapes and Gardens

IT'S NOT A HOME UNTIL IT'S PLANTED

Easy-Growing Gardening Guide, Vol. 11

Melinda R. Cordell

ISBN: 9781792177408

For more information (and books!), visit
www.melindacordell.com

Subscribe to my newsletter
and get a free gardening book:
https://www.subscribepage.com/garden

ALL THE BOOKS I'VE WRITTEN SO FAR

The Easy-Growing Gardening Series
Don't Throw in the Trowel: Vegetable Gardening Month by Month
Rose to the Occasion: An Easy-Growing Guide to Rose Gardening
If You're a Tomato, I'll Ketchup With You: Tomato Gardening Tips and Tricks
Perennial Classics: Planting and Growing Great Perennial Gardens
Petal to the Metal: Growing Gorgeous Houseplants
Gardening Month by Month: Tips for Great Flowers, Vegetables, & Houseplants
Leave Me A Lawn: Lawn Care for Tired Gardeners
Japanese Beetles and Grubs: Trap, Spray, Control Them
Stay Grounded: Soil Building for Sustainable Gardens
Genius Gardening Hacks: Tips and Fixes for the Creative Gardener
Design of the Times: How to Plan Glorious Landscapes and Gardens

Civil War Books
Courageous Women of the Civil War: Soldiers, Spies, Medics, and More (Chicago Review Press, 2016)
Gentlemen, Accept This Facial Hair Challenge! Epic Beards and Moustaches of the Civil War

The Dragonriders of Skala series (written with Pauline Creeden)
The Flame of Battle
A Fire of Roses
A Crown of Flames
A Whisper of Smoke – Get this one for free!

Young Adult Novels
Angel in the Whirlwind
Butterfly Chaos
Those Black Wings
Why Can't My Life Be a Romance Novel? A goofy romantic short
Fifteen Inches Tall and Bulletproof: Ten Short Stories

The White Oak Chronicles:
The Chieftain (a stand-alone prequel)
Outlander's Scar
Wandering Stars
Silverlady Descends

"Novels and gardens," she says. "I like to move from plot to plot."

-- Bill Richardson, *Bachelor Brothers' Bed & Breakfast*

Introduction

Style: Everybody has it but nobody really knows what it is. And when it comes to garden design, everybody has style. Sometimes, though, they have just haven't figured out what their style is.

Some people lean more toward traditional gardens with flowers to cram them into. Others enjoy formal gardens and parterres in a world of order. Or, some might find delight in a tropical garden style with all its orange and yellows and cannas and lush leaves. And some like to mix styles in a fun pastiche of plants and colors.

What do *you* like? Maybe at this time you don't know. But you eventually figure out ideas from poking around the world of plants and styles and colors and shapes and forms.

This book is written for the do it yourselfers, the DIY folks, who like to be puttering around in a garden and have dirt under their fingernails that won't entirely go away even when they scrub and scrub. These folks have rough, chapped skin along the outside of their index finger from pulling weeds – though this probably doesn't apply to those who keep their gloves on while gardening.

This is also for the gardeners with smaller budgets. Times are tough, and the hell of it is, times going to get even tougher. So if you can't afford a huge garden, this book will show a few ways to design a garden that doesn't take a lot of money and time (especially if you're working a full-time job with a side gig to make ends meet). This book is also for those with means, since there will be plenty of good suggestions for you guys to play with as well.

This book is especially for those gardeners who take an earth-friendly approach, those who are a little more laid-back in the garden, and those who are a little more informal in their approach to plants and design. My style tends to be natural, organic, and forgiving. If things get messy once in a while, it's okay, because we're all human.

There's one area where I won't compromise, and that's with the garden's soil. I believe that a garden is only as good as its soil, and organic means of disease and pest control is best. Also, we must start concentrating on landscaping styles that match the environment we're actually living in – for instance, using desert plants in a desert instead of lush, water-hungry landscapes. "Sustainability" is a word that's being bandied about a lot, but all of us need to work more closely with the natural world around us. It's a good way of living. We need to be doing better for the world we live in, the world we share with the creatures in it.

Finally, I also like to have fun in the garden. I hope this book makes you feel like you can also enjoy yourself out there. There is always room for mistakes in the garden – and believe me, when you're working with any kind of living creatures, including plants. Even plants have a mind of their own and they don't always grow the way you want them to. That's okay. It's all part of the learning process.

Anyway, if a plant is being a complete jerk, you can always dig the offender up and plant him back in a hidden corner in the garden where he won't be any trouble. Too bad you can't do that with some people.

Sometimes life gets in the way.

At those times when life gets in the way, just remember that a haphazard garden is better than no garden at all. Gardening is great, but when life is too busy, you garden will go by the wayside. That's okay. The garden will be fine – it will wait for you, to some extent.

Try not to bite off more than you can chew in the garden. Spring is an infinitely exciting time. I'm speaking for myself, but once the trees and grass start greening up and I walk into a greenhouse and that smell of peat and growing hits my nose, oh man, then I want to start picking up plants and carting them home by the truckload. My garden tends to be a wreck because of this. These days, I've been spending a lot more time at the writing desk instead of in the garden. As a result, my poor garden is even more of a wreck.

That dismayed face when somebody tells me, "Wow, Melinda, I bet you have a beautiful garden!"

The best way to start a garden is to do a self-assessment. If you tend to start projects and then keep powering through until you're done, then knock yourself out and plant whatever you like.

On the other hand, if you're like me, and you tend to wander off when you're working on something you need to finish – okay, then definitely start small. A small garden patch still gives a lot of pleasure at the end of the day.

Note: Though the garden design tips in this book should work in gardens all over the world, my plant recommendations are mainly written from my knowledge of what works in a temperate garden in the Midwestern United States – specifically, zones 5 to 6 in Missouri. For those of you who live elsewhere in the world, we have four seasons which includes a hot, dry, humid summer with temperatures from 80 to 90 degrees. Our winters are cold enough to give plants a period of dormancy, with temperatures averaging 30 or 40 degrees. If you live in a area with similar weather, you should be fine.

Save Time & Trouble With Garden Journals

(swiped from *Don't Throw in the Trowel: Vegetable Gardening Month by Month*.)

I'm putting this chapter here because I will be referring to garden notebooks all through this book. "Why is this woman so obsessed with notebooks!" the reader might cry. Well, this is partly because I've been carrying a notebook around since I was in high school. But the other reason is that gardening notebooks saved my sanity when I was a city horticulturist.

This article contains probably some of the best gardening advice you're going to get. I don't like to brag. On the other hand, it's not bragging if it's the truth.

When I worked as a municipal horticulturist, I took care of twelve high-maintenance gardens, and a number of smaller ones, over I-don't-know-how-many square miles of city, plus several hundred small trees, an insane number of shrubs, a greenhouse, and whatever else the bosses threw at me. I had to find a way to stay organized besides waking up at 3 a.m. to make extensive lists. My solution: keep a garden journal.

Vegetable gardeners with an organized journal can take control of production and yields. Whether you have a large garden or a small organic farm, it certainly helps to keep track of everything in order to beat the pests, make the most of your harvest, and keep up with spraying and fertilizing.

Keeping a garden journal reduces stress because your overtaxed brain won't have to carry around all those lists. It saves time by keeping you focused. Writing sharpens the mind, helps it to retain more information, and opens your eyes to the world around you.

My journal is a small five-section notebook, college ruled, and I leave it open to the page I'm working on at the time. The only drawback with a spiral notebook is that after a season or two I have to thumb through a lot of pages to find an earlier comment. A small three-ring binder with five separators would do the trick, too. If you wish, you can take out pages at the end of each season and file them in a master notebook.

I keep two notebooks – one for ornamentals and one for vegetables. However, you might prefer to pile everything into one notebook. Do what feels comfortable to you.

These are the five sections I divide my notebooks into – though you might use different classifications, or put them in different orders. Don't sweat it; this ain't brain surgery.

Feel free to experiment. You'll eventually settle into the form that suits you best.

First section: To-do lists.

This is pretty self-explanatory: you write a list, you cross off almost everything on it, you make a new list.

When I worked as horticulturist, I did these lists monthly. I'd visit all the gardens I took care of. After looking at anything left unfinished on the previous month's list, and looking at the garden to see what else needed to be done, I made a new, comprehensive list.

Use one page of the to-do section for reminders of things you need to do next season. If it's summer, and you think of some chores you'll need to do this fall, make a FALL page and write them down. Doing this has saved me lots of headaches.

Second section: Reference lists.

These are lists that you'll refer back to on occasion.

For example, I'd keep a list of all the yews in the parks system that needed trimmed, a list of all gardens that needed weekly waterings, a list of all places that needed sprayed for bagworms, a list of all the roses that needed to be babied, etc.

I would also keep my running lists in this section, too – lists I keep adding to. For instance, I kept a list of when different vegetables were ready for harvest – even vegetables I didn't grow, as my friends and relatives reported to me. Then, when I made a plan for my veggie garden, I would look at the list to get an idea of when these plants finished up, and I could figure out when I could take them out and put in a new crop. I also had a list of "seed-to-harvest" times, so I could give each crop enough time to make the harvest date before frost.

You can also keep a wish list – plants and vegetables you'd like to have in your garden.

Third section: Tracking progress.

This is a weekly (or, "whenever it occurs to me to write about it") section as well.

If you plant seeds in a greenhouse, keep track of what seeds you order, when you plant them, when they germinate, how many plants you transplant (and how many survive to maturity), and so forth.

When you finish up in the greenhouse, use these pages to look back and record your thoughts – "I will never again try to start vinca from seeds! Never!! Never!!!" Then you don't annoy yourself by forgetting and buying vinca seeds next year.

You can do the same thing when you move on to the vegetable garden – what dates you tilled the ground, planted the seeds, when they germinated, and so forth. Make notes on yields and how everything tasted. "The yellow crooknecks were definitely not what I'd hoped for. Try yellow zucchini next year."

Be sure to write a vegetable garden overview at season's end, too. "Next year, for goodness' sake, get some 8-foot poles for the beans! Also, drive the poles deeper into the ground so they don't fall over during thunderstorms."

During the winter, you can look back on this section and see ways you can improve your yields and harvest ("The dehydrator worked great on the apples!"), and you can see which of your experiments worked.

Fourth section: Details of the natural world.

When keeping a journal, don't limit yourself to what's going on in your garden. Track events in the natural world, too. Write down when the poplars start shedding cotton or when the Queen's Anne Lace blooms.

You've heard old gardening maxims such as "plant corn when oak leaves are the size of a squirrel's ear," or "prune roses when the forsythia blooms." If the spring has been especially cold and everything's behind, you can rely on nature's cues instead of a calendar when planting or preventing disease outbreaks.

Also, by setting down specific events, you can look at the journal later and say, "Oh, I can expect little caterpillars to attack the indigo plant when the 'Johnson's Blue' geranium is blooming." Then next year, when you notice the buds on your geraniums, you can look at your indigo plant, seek out the caterpillar eggs, and squish them before they hatch. An ounce of prevention, see?

When I read back over this section of the journal, patterns start to emerge. I noticed that Stargazer lilies bloom just as the major heat begins. This is no mere coincidence: It's happened for the last three years! So now when I see the large buds on the lilies, I give the air conditioner a quick checkup.

Fifth section: Notes and comments.

This is more like the journal that most people think of as being a journal – here, you just talk about the garden, mull over how things are looking, or grouse about those supposedly blight-resistant tomatoes that decided to be contrary and keel over from blight.

I generally put a date on each entry, then ramble on about any old thing. You can write a description of the garden at sunset, sketch your peppers, or keep track of the habits of bugs you see crawling around in the plants. This ain't art, this is just fun stuff (which, in the end, yields great dividends).

Maybe you've been to a garden talk on the habits of Asian melons and you need a place to put your notes. Put them here!

This is a good place to put garden plans, too. Years later I run into them again and find a bunch of neat ideas I haven't tried yet.

Get a calendar.

When December rolls around, get next year's calendar and the gardening journal and sit down at the kitchen table. Using last year's notes, mark events on the calendar to watch out for – when the tomatoes first ripen, when the summer heat starts to break, and when you expect certain insects to attack. In the upcoming year, you just look at the calendar and say, "Well, the squash bugs will be hatching soon," so you put on your garden gloves and start smashing the little rafts of red eggs on the plants.

A garden journal can be a fount of information, a source of memories, and most of all, a way to keep organized. Who knew that a little spiral notebook could do so much?

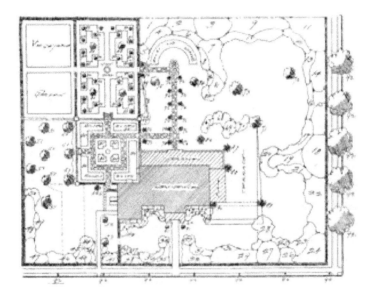

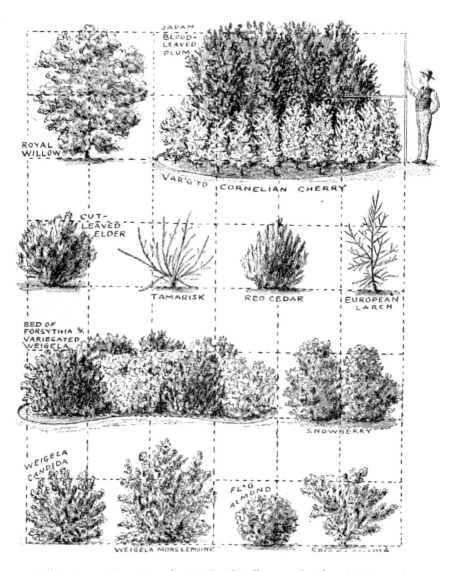

Labels in illustration: JAPAN BLOOD-LEAVED PLUM, ROYAL WILLOW, VAR'G'TD CORNELIAN CHERRY, CUT-LEAVED ELDER, TAMARISK, RED CEDAR, EUROPEAN LARCH, BED OF FORSYTHIA & VARIEGATED WEIGELA, SNOWBERRY, WEIGELA CANDIDA, FL'G ALMOND, WEIGELA MONS LEMOINE

Is this size guide written for England? All our red cedars in Missouri are much taller than that.

Before You Start Designing

What do you want from your garden? What are you dreaming of?

Do you need spaces to entertain friends, or relax, or to cook out?

Do your kids need a place to play?

Do you need a storage area?

What do you want to do with your yard? Would you like to have a peaceful spot to decompress after a busy day? Do you want to impress your neighbors with your gardening acumen? Do you want to grow vegetables? Propagate roses? Have an outdoor room for guests?

Maybe you are starting a new garden, or you're simply wanting to renovate an existing garden. This work is scary, but also exhilarating – because the possibilities seem endless.

Make a wish list!

In the previous chapter, I talked about keeping a garden notebook. Your wish list could be one of the running lists you keep in this notebook. However you prefer to do this, be sure to jot down your wish list ideas as they come to you.

"Look sharply after your thoughts. They come unlooked for, like a new bird seen on your trees, and, if you turn to your usual task, disappear; and you shall never find that perception again; never, I say – but perhaps years, ages, and I know not what events and worlds may lie between you and its return!"

Thus spake Emerson. Heed his warning!! Write down all those thoughts in your gardening notebook.

How much garden can you manage?

If you're a beginner, start small. You can always make the garden bed bigger if you are really crazy about gardening. Otherwise, if your interest wanes – or if some unexpected life event comes up that makes taking care of your garden difficult – then your garden is still manageable. It's easier to expand a garden than to make it smaller. Also, gardening is easier if you're not overwhelmed by it. Trust me.

When you are planning your garden, don't forget to put it in a place where you can see and enjoy it. Look through your kitchen window, and consider the view from your deck or upstairs window. If you can place your where you can easily look out and enjoy it, you're in business. Bonus points if you can place the garden close enough to a window so you can plant a fragrant rose right there and enjoy its scent.

Assess what you have.

Consider other aspects of your yard and house. Are there any lovely views that you want to keep? Are there other places that you want to hide from view? Do you want privacy in your yard? Do you need a windbreak to stop prevailing winds – or an opening that lets the cool wind in?

Look at your house from the street, and from behind your back property line. Do you need some large trees to shade your home? Will any corners of your house need to be softened through plants or shrubs?

While you're thinking about these issues, here are some other considerations for your property.

Are there low-lying areas where you need to fix the drainage?

What trees and existing plantings do you want to keep in the new plan? Are there any that you want to remove?

Keep in mind your local conditions and make sure the plants you want to grow fit with these conditions. An English garden with English plants would be difficult to grow in Missouri – just as a prairie garden would be difficult to grow in England. Also, you're not going to get a lush landscape in Arizona – and with the water supply being what it is, I strongly recommend using heat- and drought-tolerant plants that are native to Arizona.

For best results, consider using local native plants when you can. These are always the best plants for your area, as far as I'm concerned.

Assess what your site and soil offers.

If you're creating a brand-new garden, you'll need to figure out what your garden spot has to offer. Is it a shady spot or sunny, or a mix of both? What kinds of plants grow there now? If you see a lush grass growing thickly in the sun, this is probably a full-sun location with fertile soil. If you see ground ivy growing, or English ivy, or grass that's sparse because of the shade, then use that area for a shade garden. If nothing is growing there because the shade is too dense, you'd better find another spot for your plants, or trim off some limbs to let in some more light.

Also, look at how much water the area gets. Does water linger in puddles here long after a rain? Or, does it seem that you can never water this area enough because the soil is so sandy?

Here's how you can check the drainage of the soil. Dig a hole 12 inches wide and a little over 12 inches deep. Fill it with water. If the water drains within 10 minutes, then your soil is too well-drained! It will need to be amended with loam or compost to help hold the water in.

If the water drains within 30 minutes, it's a well-drained soil – keep that in consideration when you're choosing your plants.

If it takes from 30 minutes to four hours for the water to drain, then your soil drainage is just fine. Good for you!

If it takes longer than four hours for the hole to drain, you have boggy soil. You might consider building raised beds for your plants, or you should install water-loving plants such as rushes, cattails, and certain irises.

Note: Obviously, don't try this test if you've already had a ton of rain, or if it's flood season – then this test won't be much good.

If you do have a puddly place in the place where you're dead set on having a garden, you can either fill in the hole with some good compost, or make the best of a bad situation by putting a birdbath, small water feature, or even make a mud puddle for butterflies to drink at and add in some butterfly garden features there.

You can fix clay soils and sandy soils by adding compost. If your soil is especially problematic, install raised beds and fill them with potting soil and compost, then plant.

As you've making notes on your gardening site, look at the slope. Ideally, the ground should slope from the middle of the garden down to the front, so that water will not puddle right in the middle of your garden.

If you are planting on the side of a hill, consider how to set up the garden to keep erosion to a minimum. I don't know if you've heard of terrace farming, but it's a way farmers set up their field to keep erosion to a minimum. There are no uphill or downhill lines in these fields – only horizontal lines, or furrows, or terraces. Follow the same setup in your garden, setting it from one side of the slope to the other, instead of going straight down the slope.

If the slope is very bad, groundcovers are a possibility. If you are so inclined, an alpine or rock garden would work nicely, so you still can have your perennials AND you will have good erosion control, and one less slope to mow (and fall down). So there is that.

Remove old worn-out shrubs

If you're planning to take out those old yews and barberries, or whatever shrubs were put in for foundation plantings, be prepared for a some heavy work. Digging out an old yew takes a lot of work, to get down under the roots far enough to cut it out. When I had a job in landscape installation, there was one particularly large yew that just would not come out. We'd dug a hole that was a good four feet wide and the roots were wide and thick. I believe a pickax was involved in this operation, various saws, and even then we had about three people rocking the stump back and forth. We'd lean it hard to the right, and try to saw out what roots we could get from that angle, then we'd lean it hard to the left and repeat the operation.

Finally we managed to wrest that thing out of there and there was celebration all around.

So, in short, yew bushes can be a bear to deal with. If you're buff and tough, and you don't mind a lot of digging, AND you have a good quality saw, then knock yourself out. (Not literally – I hope.) Otherwise, hire a contractor to remove your shrubs.

Selecting Your Garden Site

What is your house style?

Rule of thumb: Your garden should match the style of the house. So if you have a modern house, then you should create a garden with a modern look.

However, at the same time, if your heart is set on an English garden in all its glorious, rambunctious mess of flowers, then you can certainly find ways to design a garden that blends the best of the old and the new.

Measure your yard.

Find a couple of sheets of graph paper for your design. Then measure out your house. The easiest way is to get a measuring wheel at the local hardware store. A good-quality wheel will cost more. However, when I worked as a horticulturist, I used a portable one with a tiny wheel and a number ticker on it. The handle telescoped down so you could stow it in the toolbox. I used this measuring wheel most of all, since I always had it handy in the city truck.

An open-reel measuring tape also works. Basically anything that can measure a whole yard is what you need.

Here's a little trick: If you want to be really precise, go to Google Maps and type in your address. Once you've adjusted the map, switch over to "Satellite" and zoom in until you see what your house and environs looks like from the air. Get as close as you can, take a screenshot, and print it out. Then you can go ahead and get measurements of your yard, your house, etc., and put them on here. Now you have measurements and an accurate map of your yard.

You can use this map when making a rough layout of your garden plan, so you can have a good idea of how what you want will fit in with the rest of the yard.

If you aren't as computer-savvy, or if you think Google is an evil corporation which has broken every law of privacy in the world (they have), then you can measure everything in the old-fashioned way.

Start with a plain sheet of paper, jotting down measurements as you go. Start with the house, the garage, outbuildings, driveway, sidewalks, decks, the placement of trees and shrubs on the property, the patio, etc.

Now, keep in mind that you should measure the whole yard ONLY if you are undertaking a large project. If you are fixing to just plant a small bed along the side of the house, don't worry about the whole rest of the yard. There's no using in driving yourself to distraction when you don't need it!

While you're walking around measuring everything, take note of the conditions in the place where you want to plant. How does the sun look here? are you getting any shade where you are? Sometimes one assumes certain ideas about an area of the yard – until you go out there and actually spend some time there.

If you don't want to plant next to the house, consider a border along a fence or your sidewalk. Another possibility is an island bed in the middle of your lawn, perhaps tied to one of your trees.

Also, consider the backdrop of your flower bed. If you have a nice wall to place it against, or a picket fence, consider putting it there, to give some visual contrast to your flowers, and also to give the design an anchor. A row of evergreens or a tidy hedge is also nice.

If you go with an island bed, you can have a tree in the center or on one side or the other, in order to provide height, color, and an anchor in the visual composition of the design.

If you are planting next to a wall, building, or fence, put some space between the plants and the structure. First, this allows air to circulate behind the plants and helps to keep plant diseases like powdery mildew, blackspot, or other fungal diseases down. Also, a space behind the border allows you to squeeze back there and clean up the plants and keep up with maintenance, which is also important to plant health, and of course to the overall look of the plant border. A two-foot space is ideal so you don't get tangled up in your own plants.

How wide should the border be?

Getting in and around the border in order to take care of the plants in it is important. If you make the border too wide or large, it's going to be tougher to maintain. Generally, a border that is two to three feet wide works just fine. If you are a dedicated gardener, the old-fashioned English perennial borders were about six to eight feet wide, which allowed you to put in plants of all heights and sizes, with big plants at the back and smaller plants in the front, and you could fit in huge drifts of flowers, which allowed for nearly continuous bloom.

Now some folks get really excited about gardening and eventually end up with a yard full of garden, with little paths winding here and there and all kinds of cool flowers, shrubs, and trees. Don't be discouraged if you can't attain this level of gardentude. Whatever you can maintain comfortably is best.

THE BEAUTIFUL FLOWER GARDEN.

BY THE WELL-KNOWN BOSTON ARTIST,
F. SCHUYLER MATHEWS,
IN COLLABORATION WITH ARTHUR FEWKS,
OF NEWTON HIGHLANDS, MASS.

We are confident this new book will mark an epoch in artistic flower-gardening, to which people everywhere are turning such close attention. Art is simple and natural;—yet where is a teacher more needed than in simple, natural arrangement? There are many gardens laid out with evident care, yet even in these it must be admitted that something is lacking, and MR. MATHEWS says, "all will agree with me that this something is *art* in gardening." Who is better able to tell us what properly pertains to the subject than a trained artist who is also an enthusiastic amateur gardener? The pages are literally overflowing with pen-and-ink sketches made from nature, so that the veriest novice may easily learn to arrange plants and flowers harmoniously. The artist-author has drawn from the best in the artistic world of gardening, showing the influence of the formal English style, also that of the Italian renaissance period, not overlooking the influence exerted by the Japanese, who are a wonderfully artistic people.

Above everything, harmony should rule in the garden; all nature proclaims the principle: "art itself is nature." Therefore, the most elaborate attention is given by the author to making plain the principles of harmony.

Not the least important part of this valuable book is that devoted to the careful description of flowers which may be easily procured and grown from seeds, bulbs, and cuttings. Bright sketches show the form and habit of growth of each class. The closing chapters are devoted to careful cultural directions by ARTHUR FEWKS, a professional grower of wide reputation. All the works previously published on this subject are elaborate and expensive, treating for the most part of the management of great estates and parks; this book is for the million seeking to surround their homes with nature in her charming moods. We therefore consider it to our interest to make the price actually less than the cost per copy for the first edition.

Finely illustrated, and in handsomely designed covers.
Price 50 cts., postpaid.

CAN BE ORDERED FROM THE PUBLISHERS, OR
ANY BOOK STORE IN THE UNITED STATES.

Published by W. ATLEE BURPEE & CO., Philadelphia, Pa.

Garden Design ... And You.

On Creativity
(Spoiler: You already have it)

When I was reading my usual pile of articles and books while researching this topic, I read about some pretentious garden writer who said, of gardens, that a real work of art is not something that could be copied or analyzed.

I see this notion quite often in the literary world as well. There's always some guy out there saying that creativity is "god-given." This guy will tell you that you can't really teach "writing" or "art" or "design." This guy will tell you that genius just happens – but not to you – and you haven't a chance of learning genius, or creativity, because these abilities not really teachable.

Let's pause here to do a thought experiment.

Let's say we're at a place where there are a lot of cattle, like a feedlot. As a result, there's also a great deal of compostable material here.

Now, imagine you're standing in this feedlot, and you take a deep breath.

Smell that?

That's the smell of everything that guy is telling you.

Of *course* art can be taught. Of *course* you can develop creativity. What's more, a plumber can be just as creative as an artist. Or a mechanic. Or a teacher.

Creativity is not exclusive to only a certain class of people – though, to be sure, those who have wealth and means to study with great teachers and in exclusive programs certainly have a head start over the rest of us. But people – specifically, people like that pretentious guy – want you to believe that they are better than you are, by pretending they are inherently superior through their creativity, aka genius. These kind of people don't like to mention their special advantages that they've taken due to wealth or who they know.

And every person, whatever their trade, can be creative. You can be creative if you're a mechanic, or plumber, or some rosarian working in the field with a bunch of grumpy roses. Creativity is not elitist. Every human tackling a problem has an opportunity to be creative. They don't always take it (some folks are a little scared of creativity), but at any rate, the muse doesn't exclusively visit artists. There are plenty of blue-collar muses in the world for all of us.

Long story short: you are a creative being, and you can indeed learn all about the things you love, and you can be damned good at them.

Oftentimes, learning creativity is simply done through getting your hands dirty in the garden. If you're out there in the garden, trying new plants, messing with design in your garden, looking at other gardens to see what works and what doesn't – and figuring out why things work (or don't)

– and you're reading gardening books, and wandering around botanical gardens, and taking notes, and talking to other gardeners, and just enjoying the process ... if you're doing these things, then you're developing your techniques and skills. Creativity grows with that.

The more you learn, the more you can do with what you learn.

> Yet all experience is an arch wherethro'
> Gleams that untravell'd world whose margin fades
> For ever and forever when I move.

Of course, everything I just said translates into whichever field of study you want to apply yourself to. Curiosity, persistence, and love are all very helpful in this as well.

Imitation – The Sincerest Form of Learning

Every artist has multiple teachers, but every artist also starts out by copying others. I didn't realize, as a gardener starting out, that I could imitate other gardeners. I read a lot about English gardening, and when I made Memorial Day boxes at the greenhouse, I often did a couple of all-white boxes, thinking about the all-white garden at Sissinghurst. (The colors in the white flowers are subtle, but actually show up fairly well when the other flowers are white as well – because white flowers often have a tinge of blue, or pink, or yellow in them that these groupings seem to bring out very nicely.)

I'd try different pairings in my garden that I'd seen pictures of in a book somewhere, but it never occurred to me to try and imitate one of Gertrude Jekyll's gardens, or Vita Sackville-West's gardens. I wish I had!

Your gardening notebook is going to be a great help in this. Tuck it in your purse or pocket or under your arm when you visit a botanical garden, or a friend's garden, or when you go to the nursery. Or keep these notes and pictures in a file on your phone. When you see a great combination, take a picture of it, and make a note of the plants in your book. Or simply make a sketch of the garden arrangement, even if the sketch consists of circles with plant names in the middle. When you write out what other people have done, the idea sticks in your brain. When it's also in your notebook, it snags your memory very neatly. Then you can go back to it later and play with it.

Of course, an appreciation for art, for photography, will help sharpen your eye for color, form, and composition, all of which will play a part in developing your garden.

Painters have paints; gardeners have plants.

But the trick here is that the artist's colors, once placed upon the canvas in their final form, will stay put. The gardener's medium is living things. When you're working with living things, you have a whole different set of challenges. Living things catch diseases, or they might show stunted growth after a big drought, or sulk, or bloom at the wrong time – or they might just keel over and die.

Van Gogh didn't have to worry about a patch of purple on his canvas catching blackspot or being eaten by bugs. And that … was probably a good thing.

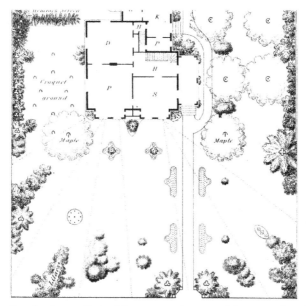

Protip: For best results, add a croquet ground to every landscape.

The Elements of Landscape Design

Every landscape design has a great variety of elements to play with, all of which you can work with to make your garden neat and exciting. These elements, naturally, are also a great part of the visual arts, and go into the composition of any painting, a work of sculpture, or architecture. People respond to these elements of design without knowing it. They look at a work of art, or walk into a beautifully built house, or sit down in a lovely garden, and they like the experience without being able to articulate why.

A very good design leads to a sublime experience. If you're able to create a beautiful and elegant design, you're more likely to enjoy your garden.

Lines

Line is one of the most important part of design, architecture, and art in general. Lines in a fine painting help unify the composition, and the same goes for architecture. Lines create all forms and patterns in your landscape, so pay attention to how you're using them.

In the landscape, a line is created by the edge of two materials – say, the edge of a garden bed, or where your landscape pavers meet the lawn. Lines are also created by the outline or silhouette of a form – for instance, the lines of a corkscrew willow in winter, with its twisted branches against the landscape. Line is also created by materials, such as a fence, a pool, or a walkway. Lines can be straight, curvy, and squiggly.

Straight lines are structural and forceful, more formal, and should lead the eye to a focal point (a statue, a tree, etc.). Curved lines are informal and relaxed, more asymmetrical. They add mystery to your space by creating views. Vertical lines move the eye up and make your space feel larger.

When you study an effective work of art or photography, you'll realize that the elements of the picture will draw your eye across it in specific ways. You'll realize that there are lines hidden and disguised in the picture that ground the picture and give it a satisfying feel – lines that give your eye a direction to travel through the painting. In some ways, line is used by artists the way authors use theme in their stories, as a unifying element.

Lines in the garden are the same way. You can use lines in the garden to control where the eye travels, or even where your body travels. A walkway is a type of line, after all.

If you need to place a pool, or a wall, or a walkway, have it run parallel to other lines in the composition. If you find the lines that are running through your garden design, you can unify them to create a cohesive look. The edge of a garden, or a line of trees, can all be used. A designer with a good sense of how these lines can be used is a gem.

Color

This is usually the part that most people first think of when they think of garden design. Of course, the flowers are a big part of color – but this also means that color is a temporary element, often the most temporary element in your landscape!

Fortunately, you can add color in a number of other ways – though the outdoor furnishings you add, or though the colors of the leaves of the plants and grasses you plant. Some shrubs have red stems or yellow berries or white bark. Hardscape, such as pavers and fences, come in all kinds of beautiful colors that compliment your garden. You can also add color through buildings, rocks, garden furniture, or garden accents you add to the garden.

A color wheel (though in black and white)

There are a number of ways to use color. You can draw up a monochromatic color scheme, which uses one color (besides green, of course). The most famous garden that uses a monochromatic color scheme is the white garden at Sissinghurst Castle, which was designed by Vita Sackville-West and uses white, silver, grey, and green to great effect.

The best way to use color is in drifts. When you have all kinds of colors mixed together in one spot, they don't show up as well. You get spots of unexpected discord where several colors clash, and the result isn't as pleasing.

However, if you plant a large drift of plants in groups of five, seven, or twenty-one, then you immediately get a solid, unmistakable swath of color that's quite effective and gorgeous. Use larger groupings of plants when possible.

Scale

It's a good idea to make sure your landscape is in proportion to your house and the rest of the area around it. Though one website said that "If you have a low house, you don't want to put an oak tree right in the middle of your lawn just because you like oak trees."

Nonsense!! If you like oak trees, then put an oak tree right in the middle of your lawn if you want to! You'll just have to draw the plan around it – but for an oak tree, it's entirely worth it.

However, it is important to consider the scale of your garden compared to your house. Here's a picture to show you what I'm talking about. Take a look at the size of those poplar trees in relation to the house:

The trees are all out of scale to the house, dwarfing it and hiding its attractive features. The viewer sees only the trees instead of the lovely house behind them.

Also, see how close these trees are to the house? Imagine that you're standing between the poplars and the house. What a tight enclosure that would be, almost downright claustrophobic.

In a good garden design, the plants should enhance the house and its features while drawing attention away from its less attractive features.

Form

Form is the three-dimensional mass of the shapes in your garden. Form is found in hardscape and plants, and it's generally the visual element that organizes the landscape and determines the style of your garden.

Formal, geometric forms include circles and squares. Circles can be stretched into ovals, or made into half-circles. Circles are a are a strong element in the design, because the eye is drawn to the center of circles. That's why circles can be used very effectively to emphasize a focal point or to connect other forms.

Informal, natural forms take the shape of meandering lines. Meandering lines mimic rivers and streams flowing through the landscape, so these kind of lines are good for pathways, the edges of flower beds, and dry stream beds.

The plants in their groupings will create forms in the garden, and the masses that the plants create when placed together is also a form. You can also create forms with a void or a negative space between plants.

Naturally, your trees have forms as well, and each tree species can be recognized due to its unique form. Common tree forms include round, columnar, oval, pyramidal, vase-shaped, and weeping. Elms have a vase-like form, sugar maples have a round form, and a columnar English oak (*Quercus robur* 'Fastigiata') has a formal, vertical form.

A spruce tree with a pyramidal and symmetrical form. This form will change as the tree matures. If you plan to have a garden for many years, it's important to keep an eye to the future of your garden – which could go on for decades when you have long-lived plants – and consider how the changing forms of your maturing plants can change the look of your garden through the years.

If you want a formal garden, then you'll choose plants you can clip into neat and tidy shapes, and your garden composition will consist more of straight lines and established styles. If you want an English or natural garden, you'll choose cheerful plants that will lean all over each other and relax into the landscape, plants in a more carefree form.

Texture

Texture in plants is what the eye can "feel" when it looks at them. Plants with a fine texture would include small-leaved plants with thin stems, such as a honey locust. Thin, strappy leaves, as those on willows or grasses, and tall, thin stems are finely textured. Sometimes fine-textured plants actually make a strong form, because the leaves are tightly-packed, as with boxwoods, making what appears to be a solid edge. Smooth stones and glass ornaments are fine-textured. Even water is smoothly textured, if you have a reflecting pool or a fountain with a fine spray.

Plants with a coarse texture include large-leaved plants with thick stems, such as catalpa, bromeliads, elephant ears, or hydrangeas. Coarse textures also include variegated colors, thick twigs and branches, and bold, irregular forms. In the hardscape department, coarse textures include rough-cut stone, unfinished wood with knots or a raised grain, and weather-beaten construction material.

This is a tree with finely-textured leaves. Compare the texture of this tree to the prickly texture of the spruce tree on the previous page.

The peeling, exfoliating bark of river birches and paperbark maples provides texture (especially in winter gardens), as does hardscape – the materials in your walkways, patios, walls, and house. Fine pea gravel in your walkways provides a different texture than a slatted, wooden walkway, or rugged paving stones. A rough-textured pathway that is traveling across a smooth lawn would immediately draw the eye to it due to these contrasting texture.

For an appealing mix of contrasting textures, place spiky blue fescue – that is, the ornamental grass *Festuca glauca* – in a planting among smooth, slate-blue stones. Combine plants with different textured leaves in one grouping, such as fat-leaved succulents with soft, feathery grasses and ferns.

Balance

The mind likes it when it can look at a space, find a central axis, and then can find some form to the weight of the shapes around this axis.

Balance is about bringing order to the garden through proportion, and uses a real or imagined central axis. Balance is affected by plant form, color, size, and texture.

Balance is also part of whether you have a symmetrical or asymmetrical garden. A symmetrical garden is more formal, in which one side is mostly a mirror image of the other side.

An asymmetrical balance is created when the masses of plants around the central point appear to be the same in visual weight.

A very symmetrical garden, with the central axis around the statue.

Unity

Repetition can unify a garden very nicely. Elements of repetition include shapes, colors, even textures. (A fine-textured tree would be a honey locust; a coarse-textured tree would be a catalpa.) You can repeat key plants through a garden. Or colors. Or shapes, like spheres, so you have a series of boxwoods trimmed into spheres, and then a glass sphere. When you have a color or a shape that's repeated through the garden, that's considered rhythm. Theme gardens have built-in unifiers, such as the white garden at Sissinghurst that I mentioned earlier.

Enclosure

When you're creating gardens, you're playing with spaces – whether they be wide-open spaces, or garden rooms where you create a sense of enclosure and comfort. Enclosure is a huge part of design, whether in gardens or architecture. When you're working with architectural design, the terms they use to describe spaces are all built around the idea of enclosure.

Enclosures separate a house from the outdoors, or one garden room from another. But the enclosures don't need to include solid walls, and you don't need a roof overhead to create a garden room. An enclosure can be edged by a simple delineation, as simple as the place where the paving ends and the lawn begins. It can be created with a boundary, such as a fence or hedge. But in creating an enclosure, an edge that's too high might leave you feeling trapped, like those poplar trees I was talking about a few pages ago. And, on the other hand, an enclosure that's too low won't feel like an enclosure at all.

When creating an enclosing wall, a 3:1 ratio of distance to height is best. So if you want to enclose a garden area that's 21 feet wide, a seven-foot hedge on one side will give you that comfortable feeling of enclosure without having to add any other features to that outdoor room.

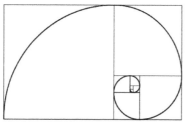

A Fibonacci spiral.

A helpful ratio

There's a mathematical principle that exists in nature and in art and architecture, and even nature itself, that allows us to create order and beauty, and it's worked for centuries. Even the inside of the nautilus shell follows this ratio, and its curves are mathematically precise and pleasing to the eye.

This principle is called the Golden Ratio, which is 1.618. One architect uses this ratio in what he calls the Golden Rectangle to lay out rectangular elements in his designs, such as lawns, patios, and garden beds. This ratio is 1 to 1.618. Mathematically speaking, the formula is ($a/b = b/a+b$).

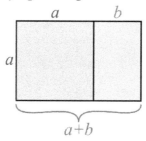

That is, you can take a square and build a rectangle next to it and that rectangle is a Golden Rectangle, one that is naturally pleasing in its proportions.

If math is not your strong suit, you can google "Golden Rectangle calculator" and get those ratios simply by typing in the size of one of the edges. So you can create a correctly-proportioned rectangular area that's 15 by 9.27 feet, or 21 by 13 feet. That way, you always have a proportionally beautiful rectangle in your garden design that always feels just right. A win!

Plant or install the big stuff first

When you start installing your garden, install the largest features first, including your trees. Once the large pieces are in, you can see where the smaller elements go and if you need to make any changes to the design before they go in. Once the big elements are in place, then you plant the shrubs, and then the perennials and groundcovers.

This is just a good rule of thumb. It's hell to plant a bunch of perennials, and then have to dig them all up because some larger element of the design is going to crash into them.

Landscape design symbols

A dot at the center of your tree denotes an existing tree. A cross at the center means that this is a proposed tree.

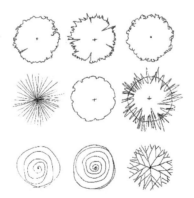

I drew these after a couple of years out of practice. It's clear that conifers are not my strong suit.

Create a Conceptual Design for Your Garden

I saw this on Erin Lau's blog and it's a damn good idea.

Take a picture of your yard. Stand where you can get the widest view of the place you want to design and take the picture there.

Then upload the photo to your photo-editing part of your computer. Use it to lighten the picture, turning down the contrast and turning up the brightness until the picture is faint enough to allow you to draw on it and see your pencil lines. Print this picture out. (Actually, print out several copies of this picture so you can make mistakes and also try out different ideas.)

Then use this printed photo to draw in the parts of the garden you'd like to keep. Once that is done, draw in the elements you want to add in – plants, trees, hardscape, outdoor furniture, etc.

Once you've played with your space through several drawings, and you've settled on an idea you like, you can lay a piece of tracing paper over the finished picture, tape it in place, then create a conceptual drawing of what your finished garden should look like.

The beauty part of this is that, if you don't like an early version of your garden design, all you have to do is print out another copy and start over. You can do multiple versions of this design – different rough drafts, different ideas – until you settle on the version you like best.

If you really would like to add some more possibilities to the process, take a photograph from the other side of the yard, and follow all the steps above. You might get a different set of garden ideas just from working from the opposite perspective! (As a writer, I do a similar thing when I'm stuck on a scene: I write it from the perspective of the scene's antagonist. By flipping a problem upside down, you can often find a solution.)

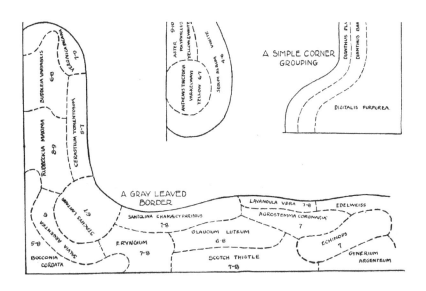

A SIMPLE CORNER
GROUPING

DIGITALIS PURPUREA

A GRAY LEAVED
BORDER

LAVANDULA VERA 7-8   EDELWEISS

SANTOLINA CHAMAECYPARISSUS
7-8

AGROSTEMMA CORONARIA
7

GLAUCIUM LUTEUM
6-8

ERYNGIUM
7-8

ECHINOPS
7

GYNERIUM
ARGENTEUM

BOCCONIA
CORDATA

SCOTCH THISTLE
7-8

Designing a Flowering Garden

A Garden is Never Finished – It Simply Evolves
(swiped from my book *Perennial Classics*)

The problem with gardening (or, the very interesting thing about gardening) is that you are dealing with living beings. Obviously these living beings can't communicate in the way we think of communication, and plants can't run away or swat the trowel out of your hand when you dig too close to their roots. Nevertheless, plants are living beings, which means they have certain whims and they definitely have ideas of their own, and they most assuredly will do their own thing. So bear this in mind when you plant what you expect is a perfect border and then the plants all sit there and make faces at you (metaphorically speaking, of course).

A garden is never finished – it keeps evolving. The short-lived plants will die out and be replaced, some plants get divided or moved around; new plants and fashions will come and go, or you'll run across some new varieties that you have to try. At any rate, the garden always changes. Even if you make a lovely plan on paper, it's still a rough draft. The garden is the final copy.

... though, in truth, you can never say that "the garden is the final copy" because the garden itself keeps evolving as well. Even if you never add anything else to the garden, the plants themselves will keep growing and blooming (or die), and some will reseed themselves with a vengeance, and of course the weeds will have their day whether you want them to or not. So even if you do nothing but maintain a garden, it will keep changing – will never be the same from one year to the next.

And besides, perennials are always moveable. If you find they don't work in one location, then dig them up and move them to a new place. Divide some of them and share 'em with your grandma.

I just said "perennials are moveable," but as always, the rule has exceptions. Plants with long taproots, like gas plant (*Dictamnus*) and indigo (*Baptisia*) aren't very happy about being moved, and will mope when you transplant them. On the whole, however, perennials are fairly cool about being dug up and moved around. Plants are generally tougher than you think they are. And if they do croak, well, get one that doesn't.

My motto as horticulturist was, "If it doesn't want to grow, well, then, it can just go away someplace and wilt." I didn't have time to baby my plants. They had to take care of themselves. I ended up figuring out pretty quickly which plants were tough and which plants were wimps. Fortunately, there are a ton of very good, easy-growing plants out there.

Don't sweat your garden plan. Nothing is perfect.

In other words, don't be like this guy.

So if you're worrying about making a perfect plan, don't. I include this information about creating a landscape plan to help you – but in this end, this is your garden. Some gardeners are "pantsers" – that is, they fly by the seats of their pants. "Hey, here are some flats of cosmos on sale – let's stick 'em in the garden! Well, there's no real good place for them, so we'll cram them behind the yarrow and let them fight it out."

My first perennial garden, which I grew during my college interregnum, was what I considered a learning garden. I was working at the nursery at the time, so I brought home all kinds of random sick plants from work, or plants I bought with my employee discount because I wanted to try it out.

That garden turned out to be a fun mess, and it was a lively jumble of blossoms, and I got a kick out of seeing how each plant grew and flowered. I considered it my learning garden, and it wasn't like I was going to invite any gardening clubs out to see it. I was having fun on my limited budget, which eventually ended up going to my college when I started going back. Them's the breaks!

So if a design right now seems like too much work, then skip it. Or simply draw a very loose sketch.

When I first started working with the Parks and Recreation department, I drew landscape plans for my gardens in winter. But when spring rolled around, I'd find that, for one reason or another, the plans always fell apart. A garden would use up all the plants that I'd intended to use in a different garden. Or there'd be a case of damping-off disease that would wipe out the trays of marigolds meant for City Hall. Or I'd see the colors together and say, "Ick," and swap out the offending plants for something better.

After a while, I gave up drawing plans. I always had a general idea of what I wanted in each garden. I kept a running list of all the colors and bloom times of the perennials and other plants already in each garden. So, when it came time to plant, I'd go into the greenhouse and see what I had available. "Felix Street Square has Nepeta, Perovskia, and Armeria on the northwest side, and the Billy Baffin roses (actually William Baffin but I was very casual with this rose). Pink and purple all over the place. Let's grab three flats of the magenta vincas. How do the pink geraniums look with the – oh my gosh, those colors are actually vibrating, put 'em back. You'd think they'd match better than that. Hey, I forgot about the Ageratum hiding over there, nice powder blue. Grab 'em all, those will look great with the pinks and purples. Hey, let's put a few drifts of the yellow Coreopsis in there, too, to make the garden pop. Come on, let's go, we're burning daylight!"

Now, granted, by the time I was city horticulturist, I had been working with plants for about 15 years, so I knew bloom times, heights, sizes, and the quirks of these plants.

Pantsing is tougher when you don't have that information already in mind. For beginners, a design is a road map – and once you have your map, you can take little side tours. A map is not an edict.

In short, have fun with the process. If something doesn't work in your garden, you can always dig it up and move it, or hide it under a birdbath, or grow vines over it.

(End of swiped chapter. Now go read *Perennial Classics*, said the author.)

Get the whole family involved with planning your garden!

Rules of (Green) Thumb for Garden Design

Once you have all your garden measured out, sit down with your graph paper, let one square equal one square foot (adjust this if you have the graph paper with the tiny squares), and start putting this all down on paper. Have the top of the paper be north, and draw a little arrow pointing that way to look more official.

As you do, you will find that you'll need to keep running out to measure more things in the yard in order to make everything line up correctly. You've measured the house and driveway, for example, but wait, how many feet do you have between the driveway and the east corner of the house? So you measure that. Where exactly does the oak tree sit in relation to the fence and the house? So you measure that. The fence and the house are not lining up correctly. So you remeasure that and try to figure out if you transposed a measurement. The oak tree seems to have inadvertently shrunk, though you'd measured it twice. Maybe it's time to take up drinking. Well, okay, but only in moderation.

Of course, that's the way the old timers did it. (Note: I am not old.) These days, you can fix up a nice landscape plan on your phone using an app, or get a more elaborate program for your laptop that will do more than just move a tree symbol around until it looks like it's placed right.

Then it's time for the big step: drawing a plan. Measure your garden. To keep your plan simple, let one-half inch equal one foot. Draw the outline of the garden on your paper.

Protip: Once you have this step finished to your satisfaction, take this paper to the copier and make several copies, and use these as the rough drafts of your garden design.

Now play with that outline. Consider the height and width of these plants. Keep short plants in front and tall plants in back, and use those pictures you've clipped (whether out of a magazine or found on the internet) to make sure the colors match. Do you want soft colors, such as purple catmint, pink petunias, and silver Artemisia? Or do you want a fiesta of red salvia and "Yellow Boy" marigolds?

Also, consider when your perennials bloom. You may love purple asters and pink sea thrift, but that color pairing won't be happening, because the asters bloom in fall and the sea thrift blooms in spring.

It's a good idea to put the tall plants in back and short plants in front. Green side up. Match the plants to the amount of sun that's available. Set your shade plants near the trees, while the full sun plants will need to be right out in the sun.

As you draw your plan, generally a good rule of thumb is to arrange them by height – tallest plants in back, shortest ones in the back. Or, as with an island bed, tallest plants in the middle, going to the shortest on the edges. But you can also blend several different varieties of plants that are the same size, the same way as you would blend several different flowers in a flower arrangement, for a good blend of colors and shapes. And you don't have to be exact on regimenting sizes. A garden isn't a lineup of soldiers on dress parade, after all.

You can arrange the plants in any way. You can arrange them in a parterre, a formal setting with neat rows, tidy edged shrubs. Or you can have a wild, natural garden with plants arranged as if they were growing wild. Chances are you will be someplace between these two extremes in your own garden.

Also, to make more of an impact, plant your perennials in drifts of 3, 5, or 7. These groups provide more of an impact than just planting one of every plant (unless you have a specimen plant that's as big as an elephant).

Protip: It's a good idea to have a little out-of-the-way place in your garden where you keep extra plants – those you've picked up when on sale but can't find a place for, plants you've picked up out of curiosity, plants you've gotten from friends and neighbors that don't quite fit into your gardening plan, or things you need to find a proper place for but haven't gotten to yet.

This little garden can get helpful, though. If you have a plant in your regular garden that suddenly croaks, you can grab a full-grown specimen from your little side garden and pop it into your regular garden, if you're so inclined, thereby filling the gap.

You can also keep your cutting garden here, so you can just pop out the back door and cut a few flowers for bouquets inside the house. Then you won't have to swipe flowers from your front gardens and leave holes in it.

Old-timey infomercials were just as bad as today's infomercials.

Always Be On the Lookout for Ideas

Designing a garden is a lot of fun. This is where you get to meet all the possibilities that are open to you. But if you're new to this, coming up with design ideas can be tough. Sometimes that's true of the old gardening pro, too! Here are a few ways to get some good ideas (and these work if you're a seasoned gardener, too).

Visit other gardens to get new ideas for plants and designs, and to see how different combinations work. If you are visiting a botanical garden, keep in mind that some of those plants might not be available to you – but you can certainly get some great ideas about form, color, and good design from these places.

Take pictures or notes of plant combinations you like as you come across them. When I see a landscape design I like, I make a sketch of it to see how it works, and figure out how

I can replicate it at home or elsewhere. Don't be shy about writing down good plant choices, or sketching garden layouts, or taking pictures of gardens with your phone.

Some magazines, books, and websites feature ready-made garden designs. Look over the design, look at the pics, and if you see some plant combination you like, write it down or download the picture. Or pick up the landscape plan for yourself, then modify it to your liking. By playing with ideas, you can come up great garden designs.

Gathering plant ideas.

Sometimes you come up with a great idea for a plant combination that you're dying to try, so you plant the flowers together in the garden – only to find out that one starts blooming two weeks before its partner does, and by the time the second plant starts blooming, the first plant is finished. Don't you just hate that?

If you refer to my chapter about keeping a gardening notebook, I mention keeping running lists for different things going on in your garden as well as events happening in the natural world.

Flip over to your running list section and start a new list: Blooming Times.

Then, all through the year, write down blooming times for every plant that you might want to use in the garden (and even those that you don't).

This is a list you can keep adding to for years and years. What you're doing here is putting down blooming times for any plant you might want to use in the garden, so you can refer back to this later to get flowering combinations that actually work for you in your area – and in your garden.

Protip: Here's a great way to keep really good track of plant colors in your garden. Go into your garden and gather a blossom from the main plants in your design (as well as a colored leaf from any variegated plants or plants with colored leaves.) Then place them all on a color copier or scanner, arrange them carefully on the glass, and make a color copy of them.

As the year passes, as new flowers come into the garden and old ones fade out, repeat this color snapshot. (When you save these pictures, or print them out, be sure to put the date on them, as these color samples will likely be different every year – indeed, every month.) Then, when you go to your local nursery, you can match the bloom times and bloom colors that you have with whatever plants they have in stock.

Good garden design uses the landscape and materials in new and creative ways. This circular garden was made from a bomb crater in England made in WWII.

"A spot that is magnificent in July may be a desert in August unless the garden is wisely planned."

Hint hint.

Design a Year-Round Garden

A year-round garden is one that has interest all through the year – not only when the flowers are blooming, but in all seasons, even in winter. There's always something interesting going on in the year-round garden, and that's the appeal of it. Creating such a garden is a challenge, but a fun one.

I really do love perennials, the workhorses of the garden. You can find a number of old-fashioned plants that can last for years and years and use them to make a long-lived garden. But if you want a good, all-season garden, mix in other kinds of plants, such as shrubs, annuals, vines, bulbs, ornamental grasses, and even small trees.

The best way to make a year-round garden is to choose plants, when possible, that provide interest for more than one season. So you'd find plants that not only have beautiful flowers, but they also offer fall color, or variegated leaves, or a striking form, or winter berries. In fact, the plant doesn't even have to flower, in the traditional sense of the term, if you plant a bed of striking ferns, or punctuate your garden with stands of ornamental grasses.

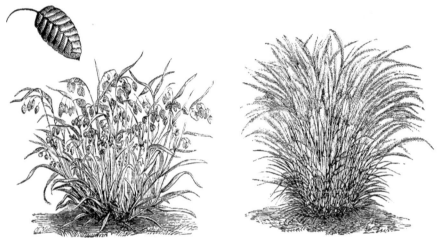

Northern sea oats (Chasmanthium latifolium) and fountaingrass (Pennisetum spp.)

These plant choices add color, form, beauty, and seasonal interest, and help fill in gaps of time when only one or two of your perennials are blooming – which happens, especially when you're just started your garden and haven't gotten all your plants synced up yet.

The key here is to mix your flowers with other elements to give your garden form, a sense of composition, but also color and interest that carries your outdoor landscape through the whole year. Even if you go out in winter, you'll still have elements in your garden that catch your eye and give you something pleasing to look at – a twisty, gnarled specimen tree, or bright red berries, each capped with snow, or a series of red-twig dogwood shrubs all looking merry against the white land, or a paperbark maple with its colorful exfoliating sienna bark.

And if you've underplanted your plants with bulbs in early spring, you can have flowers such as scilla and snowdrops and crocuses even before the snow cover is gone, before your other plants are even up and blooming.

There are a number of things you can add to the garden to give it interest all year around. Your palette is as varied as the kinds of plants you can buy.

Read on for good plant selections for each season to try in your year-round garden.

Spring

Spring is the excitement season. This is especially true after you've gone through a snowy blah winter where the whole world is white and brown and gray, and it's dark when you leave work every night, and all you get is endless gloom and cold outside. I should add that it's winter right now as I'm writing this. I have been wearing a coat constantly for the last three months, and nobody lets you hibernate if you're not a bear. It's a damn shame.

Anyway, spring is the excitement season when all the fresh green comes up and everything warms up and the spring birds come back and start building nests. And the sun is out in the spring! The wonderful warm sun!

But there's not a lot blooming in your garden in early spring, so that's when you need to add in some good spring plants to get the season started.

Trees

Early spring blooming trees include redbuds and witch hazel. Witch hazel trees, *Hamamelis* spp., bloom very early in the year, its flowers making an appearance when you're still wearing 13 layers and shivering in front of the space heater.

But at least you can look outside and see the crinkly little yellow witch hazel flowers and say "Spring's almost here!" Witch hazel is a low-maintenance, native tree that tops out at 10 to 20 feet.

Witch hazel hybrids are best for larger and more colorful blooms, as well as brilliant fall foliage in bright red and yellow. For a pretty late-winter show, plant witch hazel where the late afternoon sun will backlight their golden blossoms. For extra color, underplant this tree with hellebores, scilla, snowdrops, and cyclamen (where they're hardy). Add lilies-of-the-valley (*Convallaria*) for later in the season.

Magnolia grandiflora is a waxy-leaved magnolia. In general, the waxy-leaved magnolias are less hardy than the soft-leaved varieties, usually to zone 6. However, due to global warming, the trees can now be grown in some areas that used to be considered zone 5. Unfortunately, this cannot be considered a gain due to our planet gradually going all to hell as a result of climate change.

If you like magnolia trees, try star magnolias, *Magnolia stellata*, which are hardier than the tulip magnolias (*Magnolia x soulangiana*). A hard frost will turn the frothy pink blossoms of the tulip magnolia to brown mush, but the star magnolia keeps on blooming, unperturbed.

Magnolias are slow-growing trees, but they keep growing for decades. Slow-growing trees tend to be the trees that can hang around for a good hundred years, probably because they're built slowly and are so much stronger because of that. In the spring garden, try combining your star magnolia with some rhododendrons or azaleas, both spring-blooming shrubs, for extra brilliance.

Shrubs

Early spring blooming shrubs include old favorites like forsythia. These are now available in longer blooming varieties with brighter yellow flowers.

Pieris, also known as andromeda (*Pieris formosa* var. *forrestii),* is a shrub I kept meaning to add to various gardens, but for one reason or another never managed to do. These make an excellent show in spring. The new leaves on this plant come out bright red, fading to pink, then white, then green. The leaves almost look like flowers themselves. It makes for quite a show.

In spring – in some places, as early as March – Pieris bursts into bloom with drooping panicles of fragrant white or pink flowers that look like tiny lanterns. This shrub does prefer acidic soil, but if you can grow a magnolia tree in your yard, then you can grow a Pieris. Mulch it with a deep layer of peat or pine needles.

Dwarf fothergilla (aka mountain witch-alder) is a lovely shrub. In early spring it bears white bottle-brush flowers in profusion, and they have a soft honey scent. In fall, the foliage turns to a lovely yellow which is brushed with orange-red, and sometimes a lovely, brilliant orange-red brushed with yellow. True four-season appeal.

Early-blooming roses such as Thérèse Bugnet, Mystic Beauty, Cecile Brunner, Queen of Sweden, Reine des Violette, Felix Leclerc, and others are beauties that will give you some mid- to late-spring gorgeousness. This list of rose varieties, of course, varies from clime to clime – stop by your local rose garden in early May to see what's blooming in your area.

Noble Fumaria.　　Italian Scilla.　　Snake's-head.　　Virginian Lungwort.

Perennials

I was a perennials gal before I was a rose gal. Perennials are still one of my favorite aspects of the garden, because you plant them once and then you're done for a couple of years. Perennials are generally long-lived plants that don't require a lot of maintenance – two attributes that rank high in my book!

Brunnera macrophylla, which is often called false forget-me-nots or Siberian bugloss, is a shade-loving plant with large, heart-shaped leaves and pretty little blue flowers. This is a good, reliable perennial. These days, you can find Brunnera varieties with variegated leaves that light up your shade garden for the rest of the season after the blooms have finished. Good choices include Brunnera 'Sea Heart,' 'Variegata,' 'Alexander's Great,' the old standby 'Jack Frost,' and the form with lime-green leaves, 'Diane's Gold,' which can be grown in a sunnier location.

If you plant a forsythia bush, you can grow lungwort around it to compliment its bright yellow flowers. *Pulmonaria saccharata* is a low-growing perennial which has pretty leaves spotted with white. They bloom at about the same time as forsythia, bearing pink buds that open to sky-blue flowers – a good match with the yellow forsythia blossoms. *Pulmonaria* 'Mrs. Moon' is an old standby in the perennial garden and was one of the plants we sold when I was working in a nursery in 1993 – a couple of years ago.

A lot of old-fashioned perennials blaze brightly in spring. Columbines (*Aquilegia*) were always a favorite of mine, and I liked how the native columbines species would cross with the hybrids I planted. You never knew what to expect from the seedlings that resulted from those crosses, but the resulting flowers were often pretty cute.

Leopard's bane – *Doronicum orientale* – is a bright yellow daisy that looks great with tulips or other spring bulbs. The foliage might go dormant in summer, so plant hostas or wallflowers around the leopard's bane so you don't have a gap in your perennial garden. Apparently, according to a 1551 herbal, leopard's bane, if "layd to a scorpoine maketh hyr utterly amased and Num." So if you happen to see scorpions in your garden looking utterly amazed and numb, that's why.

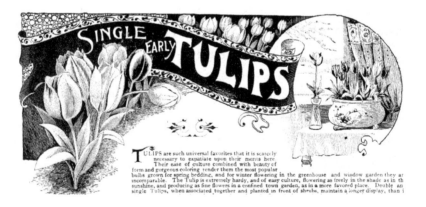

TULIPS are such universal favorites that it is scarcely necessary to expatiate upon their merits here. Their ease of culture combined with beauty of form and gorgeous coloring render them the most popular bulbs grown for spring bedding, and for winter flowering in the greenhouse and window garden they are incomparable. The Tulip is extremely hardy, and of easy culture, flowering as freely in the shade as in the sunshine, and producing as fine flowers in a confined town garden, as in a more favored place. Double and single Tulips, when associated together and planted in front of shrubs, maintain a longer display, than i

Bulbs and corms

Early-blooming bulbs such as snowdrops, crocuses, Siberian squill with its tiny flowers in the most wonderful shade of cerulean, and daffodils will help you get a jump on spring.

Tulips are one of the classic flowers of spring, and they're available in so many different varieties, species, and forms. You can get the Greigii hybrids, which have reddish-purple lines on the upper leaves and large, cuplike flowers with an eye at the center; or the small *Tulipa tarda*, which bears clusters of four or five starry flowers. Some tulips can be planted as long-lived perennials. Others, such as the exquisite 'Angelique,' which look like ruffled pink peonies, will need to be treated as annuals and replaced every year.

When I was a kid, I declared that when I was all grown up, I wanted three things always in my life: black raspberries, blueberry muffins, and daffodils in my garden. I'm afraid I've only come through on the raspberries, as I still need to get some daffodils planted. Don't let your younger self down! There's nothing happier than the first bright yellow daffodils popping up and telling you "Never fear! Spring is here!"

Underplant your early-blooming trees and shrubs with bulbs. Hostas underplanted with spring-blooming bulbs is an especially good combination. When the bulb foliage is dying off, the large hosta leaves are growing out and covering the finished bulb foliage. When the bulbs go dormant, the hostas have already taken over the area with their variegated leaves, making it look good.

Summer

Trees

I used to write for a website that sold plants in the deep south, and *Vitex agnus-castus,* known as chaste tree, was an especially noteworthy tree that sold very well there. And for good reason: Vitex is a small, multi-stemmed tree with panicles of sweetly-scented purple blossoms. The green-grey foliage, too, is scented. This little tree gets only 10 to 20 feet tall, so it's easy to tuck it into your yard where you want its fragrance and color. Vitex doesn't need much maintenance, though you'll have to trim off shoots so the tree won't turn into a shrub. (Of course, if you are so inclined you can certainly let it go shrubby.) Apparently the Vitex is also hardy up to zone 5, so I hope to see more of it in my area.

Goldenrain trees – *Koelreutaria* spp. – are a coarse-branched medium-sized tree, growing to 20 to 35 feet tall. In summer, they bear large panicles of golden yellow flowers, which are then followed by pinkish paper lanterns that later turn brown. Goldenrain trees bear deeply cut pinnate leaves that are very handsome. I liked goldenrain trees so much I planted one in the yard at my old house.

Redbuds (*Cercis* spp.) are known for their spring flowers, small purplish-pink buds that appear in April as heralds of spring. But now redbuds also add summer color with their leaves. 'Forest Pansy' as well as 'Merlot' are redbud varieties which sport maroon or burgundy leaves after the redbud flowers go to seed. 'Rising Sun' sprouts new leaves in a bright yellow that eventually fades to green.

Every time I see a European beech (*Fagus sylvatica*), I want to dig it up and take it home (an impossibility) because these trees are so graceful and stately. Beeches sport a smooth, grey trunk, and a number of beeches also have burgundy foliage, such as 'Dawyck Purple' and 'Red Obelisk.' 'Riversii' is a selection that has purple leaves in the spring that turn copper in the fall. You can also plant a tricolor beech, with purple leaves bordered with rose and white. If you are looking for a good tree to provide a striking form in the year-round garden, many weeping beech varieties are available.

Beeches seem to prefer the cooler temperatures of the north. Here in Missouri, the leaves of the variegated varieties tend to scorch in our hot temperatures. Variegated beeches tend to do better in hot locations if they have some dappled shade during the summer.

The "Upside-Down" tree at Hyde Park (Fagus sylvatica 'Pendula')

My friend Ronna has some weeping beech trees on her property, with very handsome forms and dark burgundy leaves, and I drool over them every time I go by.

Product placement: If you need some fairy gardening supplies then skip over to Ronna's website, Fairy Homes and Gardens. She has all the high-quality goods, and I've known her for years and for all that time she has been a horticultural goddess, I swear. Only much nicer.

Shrubs

In the wild, elderberries (*Sambucus nigra*) are good shrubs for birds, bearing a profusion of large platters of tiny white flowers, followed by small purple-black berries that are edible for birds and people alike (though quite seedy). I pick the berry clusters and put them in the chicken yard as treats for my hens. However, wild elderberries also spread like crazy via seeds and suckers, and is often scraggly.

Now you can get elderberry varieties that have gorgeous, wine-red leaves and a tidy habit (not "trimmed boxwood" tidy but more like "big ol' shrub that doesn't eat your yard" tidy). *Sambucus* 'Black Lace' has ferny, dark purple leaves. *Sambucus racemose* 'Sutherland's Gold' has yellow-green leaves that really remind me of sumac leaves. It can be grown as a small tree, and it bears small clusters of red berries.

Wait, wait, red berries on an elderberry? *Sambucus nigra* species have only wide plates of black berries – I have never seen red berries on them.

But then I realized that the 'Sutherland's Gold' was actually related to the European elder trees, not the American elderberries. Then it all became clear. That's why 'Sutherland's Gold' can also be grown as a small tree – the European elder trees are small trees that are common overseas. If you've read about an elder tree in fairy tales, chances are it's *Sambucus racemose*.

I'm glad I cleared that question up as it was giving me the taxonomical fits for a while. Not pleasant.

Moving on!

Sweetspire (*Itea virginica*) bears white, sweet-scented, six-inch flower spikes in summer, followed by red-purple foliage in fall. Varieties commonly available are 'Henry's Garnet,' which is a very colorful variety with purple, red, and yellow leaves in fall, and larger flowers than the original species. 'Merlot' is a dwarf sweetspire variety with striking wine-red fall color.

I will acknowledge that barberries – *Berberis* varieties – are great all-season shrubs. They sport tiny yellow flowers in spring. Their fine-leaved foliages comes in all kinds of shades. Some barberry varieties have rich, wine-red leaves, while others are a jaunty lime green that look great all summer. In fall barberries have cute little red berries that last all winter.

Here's another reason why I appreciate barberries: one time I was being chased on campus by this idiot man. I'm a fast runner but he was determined to catch me. I knew I couldn't outrun him, so I leapt over a hedge of barberries to get away from him, and then stopped to watch the fun. That idiot, thinking he had me, blundered straight into a barricade of barberry thorns. "Ow! These have thorns!" he complained, flailing around. No kidding, Sherlock. So much for him.

So barberries have very good points. The only problem is that barberries also have very *sharp* points. I've trimmed many barberry hedges in my horticultural career, and their thorns are very slim, and there's no nub at the base of the thorn to grasp to pull the thorns out of my fingers. I've spent many hours digging out barberry thorns with straight pins, and they'd range in size to bitty thorns I could hardly see, to gigantic thorns that looked large enough to go through my whole finger. Even when you wear leather gloves, those thorns will poke through the seams of the gloves and jab you.

So, that's why I personally will not plant bayberries.

Side note: Every horticulturist and gardener will have knee-jerk reactions to plants that either do or do not make sense. I still avoid sweet woodruff because we had a lot of pots at the nursery in 1993 where the plants rotted, and then I had this dream in which my cat and I were trying to sell those pots of not-so-sweet woodruff. That's the only reason. Often, our prejudices make absolutely no sense in the light of logic – and yet we cling to them for the most inane reasons.

Perennials

Ornamental grasses are good candidates for the all-seasons garden. They provide form, long-lasting color, and winter interest while being hardy and carefree.

Hakonechola is one example of an ornamental grass that really fits the bill. It's a lovely grass from Japan, where its beauty is greatly prized. It's a low, mounded grass, variegated yellow and green, and in fall produces feathery flower plumes.

Yarrow – *Achillea tomentosa* – bear large plates of golden yellow flowers in midsummer. Their feathery leaves have a silvery-grey hue that is lovely when it's not blooming. Yarrows come in all shades and colors. Paprika yarrow (*A. millefolium* 'Paprika') has paprika-colored flowers and fine, ferny leaves. Yarrows overall perform well even during hot, dry summers. You can leave the flower heads up after their blossoms are done to add interest in your winter garden.

Sea thrift, *Armeria*, is an old favorite of mine. It's a small, low growing plant that looks like a tuffet of very tidy grass. But in early summer, the little plant sends up round clusters of dark pink flowers. It's native to the shores of Britain, where it clings to the rocky cliffs above the sea and blooms like crazy. So they're also tough little plants. A sure winner.

I used to have a Japanese anemone (*Anemone hupehensis* var. *japonica*) that was covered with white blossoms in August and looked gorgeous – except then a bunch of blister beetles ate the whole plant up. Grr! I still hate blister beetles. If you live in an area without these noxious pests, then grow Japanese anemone in large drifts for the best effect. Pair them with fall-blooming azaleas.

If you have a paved path in a carefree garden, then you should have thyme – specifically, *Thymus praecox arcticus*. It's a tough little thyme that makes a low, dark green mat on the ground, which in early summer turns into a low, purple-red mat on the ground. Let it grow up in your walking path for color, and enjoy the scent of thyme that rises up when you walk on it.

Fall

Trees

Most every deciduous tree is a winner in fall. Sugar maples, white and green ash trees, red maples, sweet gum trees all deck themselves in gorgeous colors. What's more, all of these trees have new hybrids and selections on the market, all of which are bred for really intense, reliable color.

Black gum, or tupelo, *Nyssa sylvatica*, is one such tree. Tupelo is a very slow-growing tree, but its leaves turn a most amazing hue of scarlet in autumn.

Japanese birch (*Betula platyphylla* 'Whitespire') has white, peeling bark which is a handsome addition to the garden all year around, and in fall these birches make a lovely show of brilliant gold leaves. In some parts of the United States, the bronze birch borer has been a real problem for birches, but the 'Whitespire' birch is more resistant to the beetle than the hapless *B. pendula*, which the borers treat as their personal buffet. The Whitespire birch is not wholly resistant, as stressed trees can find themselves plagued by borers. Plant your birch in a place where it won't be stressed – someplace with deep soil, like a backyard. Avoid planting them in the hellstrip between the street and sidewalk. Give your birches (or indeed any tree) a place to stretch their roots out.

The perpetual favorite fall foliage tree is the sugar maple (*Acer saccharum*) with its yellow, orange, and red leaves that brighten many a street and backyard in fall. Red maples (*Acer rubrum*) turn a brilliant red all over. The quaking aspen tree (*Populus tremuloides*) in northern, cooler climates also makes a delightful show all in gold. American persimmon (*Diospyros virginiana*) leaves turn yellow-green in the north and red-purple in the south. The fruits on the trees are supposed to be delicious after frost, but I've had nothing but bad luck with them, picking only the ones that pucker my mouth inside-out. 'Woolbright' is a persimmon variety that has good fruit if you can beat the raccoons to it. (Raccoons always know when persimmons are ripe – but, since raccoons are die-hard opportunists, they might not leave you any.)

Sweetgum (*Liquidambar styraciflua*) is somewhat like maples in color except with some darker reds. Sweetgum trees will drop annoying seed capsules, but you can now purchase a sterile female cultivar called 'Rotundiloba.' However, this particular selection isn't very winter-hardy north of St. Louis – so folks in zone 5 and north are out of luck. Or, you can buy a male sweetgum tree at your local nursery.

(If those sweetgum balls are driving you nuts, call a certified arborist and have her inject a plant-growth regulator that contains indole-3-butyric acid before the flowers develop. This growth regulator will kill the flowers before they set fruit – and viola, no seed balls in the fall.)

Shrubs

Chokeberry, *Aronia arbutifolia*, bears fragrant white to light-pink flowers in spring. In fall, chokeberry trees bear a generous portion of brilliant red berries that last through the winter (and you can make jam or jelly with them). When you add in its epic, brilliant red fall color, chokecherry makes a great year-round shrub. This shrub can spread to some extent, but it's a great low-maintenance plant and looks good in naturalized masses in borders or natural settings. It is a member of the rose family, which is why its spring flowers resemble apple blossoms.

Serviceberry, *Amelanchier canadensis,* is another member of the rose family that sports white blossoms in spring, red foliage in fall, and berries in summer through winter, though these are usually eaten by robins before they make it to winter. Serviceberries can be grown as a shrub or small tree. The species can be naturalized and does well in wild areas, but if you would like a small serviceberry tree in your yard, go with one of the new varieties that are bred for show. You can get *Amelanchier laevis* varieties such as 'Cumulus', 'Prince Charles' and 'R.J. Hilton' if you'd like a lovely tree with a columnar shape. *Amelanchier x grandiflora* 'Autumn Brilliance' offers intense orange-red color in fall.

Perennials

Asters are an old favorite, though in some areas they can be an invasive species. But they come in so many different sizes, shapes, and colors, that you can create a huge drift of them by siting tall asters in the back down to dwarf aster varieties in the front. Asters are carefree and don't need much care and really can put on a show of color.

Another fall favorite is *Sedum* 'Autumn Joy.' It bears large pink flower heads which attracts all kinds of butterflies, small wasps, honeybees, and other interesting insect varieties. Sedums, commonly known as stonecrop, is a diverse species with large plants like 'Autumn Joy' as well as all kinds of groundcover-sized varieties with all different leaf colors, and they flower like crazy in season. Whatever form your sedum is in, it's a cheerful little plant, easy to care for, and it doesn't fight with its neighbors. A winner all around.

Perennial hibiscus don't have much for all-season color – they actually don't even come out of the ground until May – but their flowers in magenta, burgundy, pink, and white open up until they're the size of dinner plates. Grandma Mary saw me growing one of these and wanted to know what they were, which surprised me because grandmas know everything about plants! So it was kind of crazy to know a plant she didn't. So I got her a perennial hibiscus too, and she grew the hell out of that thing.

Bulbs and corms

Don't forget to underplant your shrubs with fall-blooming bulbs. Crocuses have a number of fine varieties that bloom in fall.

I will never in my life forget the time that I saw some pink flowers blooming in Grandma Ann's yard when I was ten years old.

"What kind of flowers are those?" I asked.

"Naked ladies," Grandma said.

And then I completely died of embarrassment.

Naked ladies are also called surprise lilies, because when your church-going grandma says the word "naked" in front of you, you are sure as hell going to be surprised.

Their scientific name is *Amaryllis belladonna*, and, like their houseplant relatives, the pink trumpetlike flowers stand at the top of a long stem. After the flowers are done, they'll grow out a bunch of long, straplike leaves for the rest of the year. You can put surprise lilies in the middle of a bunch of hostas or ground cover and let them pop up and make a nice impression on everyone. And if some kid asks you what those pretty flowers are, especially if that kiddo is heading to puberty, tell her they're surprise lilies. She'll thank you later.

Dahlias are a gorgeous plant with amazing flowers that are about the size of dinner plates. You can dig up the rhizomes every fall and store them in peat moss until next spring when you plant them again, or you can simply grow them as an annual. Dahlias come in an amazing array of shapes, forms, colors, each one more mind-boggling than the last.

Side note: Really, there's such an amazing variety of plants out in the world that it's hard to choose just one favorite. Though, when it comes down to it, this is pretty much true about most other plant species in the gardening world. The more you dig, the more there is. I like this a lot. It goes to show how the world is amazingly full of so many good things.

Okay, that's enough soapboxing out of me. Let's get back to the plants.

Winter

Trees

Specimens with exfoliating bark are a good choice for year-round beauty, but they make an especially good show in winter. River birch (*Betula nigra*) is a great, multi-stemmed tree with buff-colored peeling bark. It's a good shade tree through summer and has plenty of winter interest. Also, it's resistant to borers, which paper birch trees (including European white birch, *Betula papyrifera*) tend to be susceptible to.

For small spaces, a paperbark maple, *Acer griseum*, is a lovely choice. These are a small maple with textured, exfoliating bark in several different colors of bronze. What's more, the branches are twisty and craggy as an old oak's, like sculpture. Paperbark maples also have the bright fall colors of red and orange as other maples do – a win-win. I'm always enchanted by these little trees every time I see them.

I like ginkgos in winter because of the almost architectural form of their branches on some trees. Really, I like ginkgo trees in any season. If at any time I'm passing one of these trees, I will pluck one of the fan-shaped leaves and press it in my notebook. It's something I've always done, partly for good luck, partly because I just like the leaves. Ginkgo leaves turn a gorgeous gold in fall – unless a sudden frost hits, and then the tree will drop all of its leaves at once in a waterfall. It's startling if you're not expecting it.

Ginkgos are a very slow-growing tree, so they're more expensive because of it. If you can invest in one and have the space to grow it, do it. They'll reward you for a hundred years or even more.

Ginkgo biloba leaves and fruit

Fun fact: Ginkgos are the only tree in their order, the Ginkgoaceae, and they're a holdout from the time of the dinosaurs. Years ago when I was working at the nursery, I mentioned this fact to a couple who turned out to be evangelical Christians. They looked concerned and when we parted ways, they gave me a religious tract about how dinosaurs were a hoax and the world was created in six days just as the book of Genesis said. Ah, me!

Holly (*Ilex aquifolium*) is a good tree – unless you live on the west coast, where it has become a noxious, invasive weed. In other climates, you have a smorgasbord of hollies to choose from. Sizes range from a six-inch tall spreading dwarf to a 70-foot tall behemoth. The sky is the limit with these plants – literally.

Remember: hollies are dioecious – that is, they have male plants and female plants. If you want good berry production on your female hollies, you'll need to plant a male plant within 30 to 40 feet of them.

Shrubs

For winter interest, choose shrubs with interesting bark or colorful twigs (as with the red-twig dogwoods) and berries. Bonus points planting shrubs with berries that birds enjoy eating. Cedar waxwings seem to like honeysuckle berries.

Evergreen shrubs through the garden will help keep some green, or at least greenish colors, in your garden even when snow is thick on the ground. Plant some little boxwoods, trimmed into balls, through the garden to keep the design lively.

Of course, your holly plants are going to steal the show in winter. For great winter berry displays, plant *Ilex verticillata* 'Red Sprite' for a truckload of brilliant red berries, or *Ilex verticillata* 'Winter Gold' for golden-orange berries. Birds will eat these berries, and they often persist until spring. (As with any holly, provide one male plant within 30 to 40 feet of the female plants so they'll bear berries.)

Viburnums are good shrubs for colorful winter berries, as well as spring flowers and fall color. European cranberrybush, *Viburnum opulus*, bears bright red berries that turn into dried red raisins, while the American version, *Viburnum trilobum*, bear large clusters of red berries. You can even eat the fruit from the shrub, or make preserves.

Ornamental grasses

Add ornamental grasses to your winter garden. These come in all kinds of different forms and shapes. *Hakonechloa*, also known as Japanese forestgrass, is a yellow and green weeping grass. Blue fescue is small and spiky and bluish and cute. *Pennisetum* is about two or three feet tall with wine-red leaves and soft red foxtails. You don't have to trim back your ornamental grasses in fall – keep them to provide winter interest in your garden.

Winter is when your design will be pared down to the bare bones. This is a good time to review how your design looks and think of ways to improve the bones of the design.

Don't forget to keep a place in your design for a heated birdbath so your poor birds have something to drink when all the world is frozen.

Flowers in winter?! Sure!

In late fall, you can plant some cold-loving flowers and plants to carry your landscape into winter. Pansies are the ultimate warriors when the temperature drops, and will keep smiling even as the snow's falling on them.

Ornamental kale is also cold-hardy, and will brighten a landscape through November and even December, depending on weather.

Snapdragons stop blooming reliably somewhere in October, though their foliage will stay green through November.

Here endeth the gardening design book.

I hope this was helpful to your gardening work, and I hope you found this to be an enjoyable read.

If you have any questions, comments, or concerns, drop me an email at rosefiend@gmail.com. If you'd like to share pics of your garden, knock yourself out! I'll post them on my blog and social media.

My readers are the best readers in the world, and I'm glad to have every one of you in these books. I still get such a kick out of people reading my books! This never gets old. Thank you!

FREE PREVIEWS OF MY OTHER GARDENING BOOKS

Sample Chapter: *Don't Throw In the Trowel: Vegetable Gardening Month by Month*

Two things:

First: You know more about gardening than you think.

Second: A garden – the soil – plants – all of these are very forgiving. When it comes down to it, you can make a lot of mistakes and still come out with good results.

Don't Throw in the Trowel: Vegetable Gardening Month by Month. includes info on seeds, transplanting, growing, and harvesting, as well as diseases, garden pests, and organic gardening. I also talk about garden prep, because a good plan, a garden notebook, and a little off-season work will save you a lot of trouble down the road.

I've worked in horticulture for 20 years: in landscape design and installation, as a greenhouse tech, perennial manager, and city horticulturist & rosarian. This book shares what I've learned so far.

Planning the Vegetable Garden

It's excitement time when you grab your stacks of seed catalogs and your pencils and your big sheets of paper (or, for those of you who are savvy enough to be reading this book on a Kindle or Nook, your tablet with a landscaping app). Planning the vegetable garden is when you take all those bright ideas dancing in your head and try to put them on paper (or on a screen).

Here are a few questions to ask that will help you through the process.

What vegetables does your family like? Check with the rest of the crew to see if there are any vegetables they'd like to see on the table. Sometimes they might surprise you. So you keep planting pumpkins and making nutritious pumpkin spice everything. Have you asked the rest of your family if they want pumpkin spice everything? If they say No, then sigh dramatically but plant something else. The old saying, "everything in moderation," certainly applies here.

What do you want to get out of the garden? Do you plan to do a lot of canning/dehydrating? Are you trying to lower your food budget? Make holiday decorations? Plan (and plant) accordingly.

Always start small. A garden can end up being a daunting task. You can always expand later. Or, if there's a new vegetable you want to try out, plant just a little bit of it instead of two long rows.

How are you going to cultivate the rows? Tiller, hoe, tractor? Put enough space between the rows to allow your implement of choice to fit. An additional note: if you had a lot of trouble keeping up with weeds last year, maybe this year you might make the rows just wide enough to admit the lawnmower. No, I'm serious, that lawnmower can be a lifesaver when your garden gets out of control.

Other tips:

Put all the perennial crops (asparagus, rhubarb, strawberries) together at one end to make everything easier to manage.

You can plan for succession crop, or a fall garden, and overlap these areas. For example, after you've harvested all the radishes, plant the area with tomatoes.

After the spinach is done, plant cucumbers. That way, you can keep production going after each crop is finished.

In hilly areas, plant along the contours of the hill. Up and down planting will lead to erosion.

Plant rows running north and south. Otherwise, the plants will shade each other during the day.

Later on, make notes about what worked and what didn't, and put them in your gardening notebook for next year.

Sample Chapter from *Rose to the Occasion: An Easy-Growing Guide to Rose Gardening*

Roses are the Queen of Flowers. They're beautiful, fragrant, and elegant - and roses require all the pampering of a real Queen, don't they?

Actually, they don't!

Rose gardening can be easy and pleasant. I've worked 25 years in horticulture and cared for over 300 roses in a public rose garden when I was municipal horticulturist. I found ways to keep rose gardening fussbudgetry to a minimum while growing vigorous roses that bloomed their heads off. Rose to the Occasion: An Easy-

Growing Guide to Rose Gardening shares tricks and shortcuts that rosarians use, plus simple ways you can keep up with your to-do list in the rose garden.

Gardeners of all skill levels will find this book helpful, whether they be beginning gardeners or old rosarians, whether they have a green thumb or a brown thumb.

Rose to the Occasion is the ultimate resource for any rose gardener, or anybody in need of good gardening advice. Roses are filled with romance, history, color, and fragrance. Grow some. They are worth it.

If you like the rose book preview (below), you can find the whole, finished ebook on Kindle. If you'd rather have the paperback version of this book, you can find it at Amazon.

INTRODUCTION

When I started working as city horticulturist, I took care of a bunch of gardens around the city, including the big Krug Park rose garden. It included a bunch of the usual scrawny tea roses, some shrub roses, and a bunch of bare ground.

I was more of a perennials gal, but when I looked at the roses, some of them were really nice. The 'Carefree Delight' roses were covered with rumpled pink blossoms. There was a tall 'Mr. Lincoln' rose and some 'Double Delights' that smelled amazing. A bunch of 'Scarlet Meidilands' were really putting on a blooming show, with tiny scarlet flowers cascading all over them. Not shabby at all.

I started taking care of the roses, but along the way I noticed that a lot of the 'Scarlet Meidilands' were sprouting odd growths. Most of the new growth looked fine, with bronzed, flat leaves that looked attractive. But some of the new growth was markedly different – skinny, stunted leaves with pebbled surfaces, and hyperthorny canes that were downright rubbery. The blossoms on these shoots were crinkled and didn't open worth a darn.

I hollered at Charles Anctil, a Master Rosarian with the American Rose Society. We'd known each other since 1992 when we both worked at the Old Mill Nursery. He'd been working with roses for a good 50 years, so he knows his stuff. At any rate, Charles looked over the roses and told me that those roses, and others, had rose rosette virus, a highly contagious disease, and a death sentence for a rose. Every one of those roses had to come out. He couldn't believe the extent of the damage. He said that he had never seen so many roses infected by rose rosette in one place.

Oh great! Why do I get to be the lucky one?

I dug up many roses that spring. In winter, I got a work crew and dug up 50 more. I had to replace all those roses, so I started researching new varieties.

As city horticulturist, I was already running like hell everywhere I went, so I wanted roses that wouldn't wilt or croak or wrap themselves in blackspot every time I looked at them cross-eyed. I wanted tough roses, roses that took heat and drought and bug attacks and zombie apocalypses with aplomb and would still come out looking great and covered with scented blossoms. (And the blossoms HAD to be scented – there was no two ways about that.)

I started reading rose catalogs. I talked to Charles some more, which is always fun. Somewhere along the way, I got obsessed. I immersed myself in roses. That's how I learn – I get excited about a subject and start reading everything in sight about it, like it's a mini-course in school. I read about antique roses, which were making a comeback. Different rose breeders, most notably David Austin, were crossing modern varieties with old varieties and getting roses that combined the best of the new and the old. Other breeders were creating roses that were tough and disease-resistant.

I planted some antique roses, and they looked great. I planted more. The rose garden was really starting to look spiffy, even though I still had to take roses out every year due to the rose rosette virus. I even tucked in some annuals and perennials around the garden to doll up the place when the roses conked out in July and August.

Roses are amazing plants. Many old roses have a long and storied history. Some species that were growing during the time of the Pyramids are still blooming today. And these roses are attractive and fragrant. What could be better?

Some people say that you can't grow roses organically. I say you can. I did use a few chemicals when I was a horticulturist, but that was because I had a huge list of things to do in a limited amount of time. I used Round Up for spot-weeding (a tiny squirt for each weed, just enough to wet the leaves), a systemic granular fungicide to keep up with blackspot, and Miracle-Gro as part of the fertilizing regimen for convenience.

If you choose to use chemicals, use them responsibly. Don't spray them and expect the problem to be fixed. They work best when you combine them with other control methods. I'll give you an example that's not rose-related. I had a mandevilla in the greenhouse that had a huge mealybug problem. (Mealybugs are a small, white insect that sucks out plant juices. The young bugs look like bits of cotton. Picture to the right.) I sprayed the plant with insecticide until the leaves were dripping. The mealybugs were still there. I put a systemic insecticide around the roots of the plant and watered it in. The mealybugs didn't care.

So I just started squishing the mealybugs with my fingers, a gross job because they squirt orange goo. At that point, I didn't care. I searched them out and squashed them where they were cuddled up around buds, in the cracks of the plant, and under the leaves. I even found some on the roots just under the soil. I squished those and added a little extra potting soil. I checked the plant every other day and squished every mealybug I could find. After a while, I stopped finding them altogether. Then I fertilized the plant, and the mandevilla put out leaves like crazy and started blooming. Success!

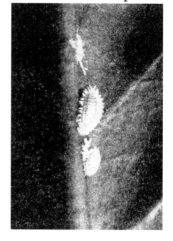

Chemicals aren't a cure-all by any means. They're convenient, but sometimes you just have to get in and do a little hands-on work with the plant to help it along. It's a good feeling when a plant you've been working with rights itself and perks up again.

Though I'm no longer a horticulturist, I wrote this book because I have worked in horticulture for about half my life, and have a decent understanding about how the natural world works. I might possibly be just a little crazy about roses. I hope my experiences are helpful and that you're able to benefit from them – and that your roses benefit as well.

ROSA RUGOSA.

Sample Chapter from Stay Grounded: Soil Building for Sustainable Gardens

One of the most important things a gardener can do is to build up the soil in her garden. But keep in mind that soil-building is not a one-time operation – it's a process. As humus is devoured by microorganisms, worms, and plants, more organic material must constantly be added in order to keep the soil biomass, and thereby the plants, well-fed and happy. Also, humus makes the soil porous and fluffy, builds a strong soil structure, and releases nutrients in a form that's easily absorbed by plant roots. Stay Grounded is your one-stop shop for soil building success.

SOIL BUILDING:
Saving the world, one dirt clod at a time.

One of the most important things a gardener can do is to build up the soil in her garden. But keep in mind that soil-building is not a one-time operation – it's a process. As humus is devoured by microorganisms, worms, and plants, more organic material must constantly be added in order to keep the soil biomass, and thereby the plants, well-fed and happy. Also, humus makes the soil porous and fluffy, builds a strong soil structure, and releases nutrients in a form that's easily absorbed by plant roots.

Chemical fertilizers will not add humus to the soil. These are merely nutritional supplements; plants and their soil need real food – organic material.

But so much good organic material never makes it back into the soil. Leaves, grass clippings, and yard waste ends up choking our landfills instead of nourishing the ground. This is wrong.

Mulch the world!

I have a fairly simple way to deal with weeds: mulch. I like to take newspapers, ten pages at a time, and lay them over the garden, making sure there's enough overlap between each section so light won't get down to the soil. Then I throw straw, grass clippings, leafmould, or whatever on top to make it all tidy and neat.

The neat thing with the newspapers is that you can get a ton of them for your purposes for free, simply by asking your neighbors or by picking them up at the local library. Also, you can lay these newspapers right over the weeds and you never hear another peep out of them for the rest of the year. Even when you have tall grass or weeds up to a foot tall, stomp them down, or mow them, before putting the newspapers on top. They get smothered right out.

The newspapers will also break down and add valuable organic material to the soil. You can lay your tomatoes right on top. You won't have to wipe the dirt off your low-hanging fruits any more. Nice, huh?

Use those leaves!

Next, use leaves and excess grass clippings in the garden. Fifteen big bags of leaves, when chewed up by a lawnmower, turn into an inch of mulch on a 15 by 25' garden. (The job took about 30 or 45 minutes.) I did that last fall; this spring, I'm finding worm castings all over!

Pour the leaves out on your garden, mow them into little pieces, and till them under. Or just leave them on top of the soil and don't bother tilling. With mulch, you don't have to worry about your garden drying out – or weeds coming up.

If you don't have leaves, take a trip to the local landfill and get some. There's usually a separate area for yard waste, and there the leaves are free for the taking. (Be careful with grass clippings, because they sometimes contain herbicides.) Or grab bags of leaves off the curb before the garbage truck arrives. Or get them from your neighbors; they're always glad to have them taken off their hands.

Earthworms = earth movers

The more I read about earthworms and observe them, the more I am convinced that these creatures are a blessing to the soil. They bring up valuable nutrients from the subsoil, their castings are among the best plant food, their tunnels bring air (which is rich in nitrogen) into the ground. Plant roots even seek out earthworm burrows for the nutrients they contain.

Nightcrawlers are best for this work. The red worms, or red wrigglers, prefer to live in compost and leafmould; they're good for mixing up cool compost piles but will not dig very far into the soil. Nightcrawlers will dig burrows deep into the ground, which is what you want.

After it rains, pick earthworms off the sidewalks to put in the garden. Or, go to the bait shop and get them there. See if they'll throw in some egg cases with your worm purchase, because if all the worms don't survive, the egg cases will. Dump a couple of worms out in various places around the garden and cover them with a little soil so they can get underground before the sun and wind dries them out. They generally will get underground within the hour, even on really cold days.

I generally put worms out in the garden every spring. Twelve to 24 worms would probably be good for a small garden, twice that for big gardens.

Green manures

Green manures such as buckwheat, clovers, lespedeza, or oats can be grown between rows, under tall plants, or at season's end all over the garden. In any case, they're tilled under three weeks before a new crop is seeded to allow them to decompose. It's a valuable way to get fast organic material.

Use green manures fill in where a crop has just finished. For example, once the spinach is all picked, throw down some rye seeds or white clover to fill the area in until next spring. Chickpeas make a nice cover crop, and they're edible, and they add much-needed nitrogen to the soil. Daikon radishes are good, too.

Grow legumes as an understory to your hungry corn crop. Leave enough space between the corn rows in order to run a lawnmower between the rows. This will keep the cover crop nice, neat, and low, and the clippings will provide lots of nitrogen-rich mulch for the rest of the garden.

Alfalfa is great for walkways because its clippings, as they break down, release a chemical called triacontanol that acts as a growth stimulant to plants. A small amount of alfalfa clippings can increase vegetable yields by 30 to 60 percent. And those alfalfa roots go deep into the subsoil, pulling up nutrients from deep underground, breaking up soil, and fixing nitrogen.

If you don't want to plant alfalfa, but you want its benefits, you can purchase alfalfa meal at feed stores or order it online. Scatter it over the soil according to package directions to improve growth. Don't spread it too heavily because it will mat and shed water.

Compost

Compost is a fine way to recycle kitchen and garden scraps into fertilizer. And it's earthworm heaven.

Kitchen scraps that are good for compost include such things as fruit and vegetable remains, eggshells, and bread. It's not a good idea to put meat products or leftover milk products in a compost pile (unless it's a very hot pile) due to the possiblities of it attracting dogs and cats. Also it could smell bad. However, if you've been fishing, you can bury the fish bits in the soil. Fish bits are high in nitrogen, and they will make your corn plants love you.

I generally throw my compostables onto the garden during the winter, and put them on the compost pile during the rest of the year. I've heard that compostables on the ground attract mice. But in deep winter they'll also attract songbirds, which is nice. (It's always fun to throw popcorn out to see what kinds of birds I get.)

Some people also dig small holes into particularly infertile areas of the garden, drop compostables into it until it's nearly full, then close it up and start a new one. This doesn't work so well in desert soils – produce buried in sandy soils has been dug up a month later, looking just as fresh as it did when it had been buried.

My soil is evil!

Sometimes you get soil that has basically been created by Satan. Examples of evil soil include subdivision soil – that pasty clay that's created by heavy equipment churning up soil, wet or dry, and compacting it into concrete. Or you have desert asphalt, or fragipan, or stuff you have to take a jackhammer to.

Raised beds are always a good idea here. Lay a thick layer of newspapers over the ground, make an enclosure, then it fill up with compost, rotted manure, and topsoil brought in from elsewhere. Go heavy on the compost! Grow a hedge of deep-rooted legumes around the outside of the enclosure, and underplant tall vegetables (like corn) with small legumes such as white clover. Release nightcrawlers into the soil. This will give you a place to plant while you wait for the compost and the earthworms to do their work on the soil underneath.

Every year, try to mix the good soil in just a little bit more, by double digging, or, if that's not working, even by moving aside the top layer of the soil and working a garden fork into the bad soil to aerate it. Keep laying down the organic material, though. Here, more than anything else, soilbuilding is a process. It will take several years of hard work to bring a dead soil back to life, so be patient.

But a living soil is the best soil for all. So keep at it.

So, keep adding humus in every way, shape, and form you can think of to keep the garden happy and to keep the soil biomass active. This will make an incredible difference in your garden – one you'll definitely love.

Me in 1995, when I embarked upon the grand adventure
of being a published author.
I was kind of a writing hotshot back then.
If you want to be perfectly honest, I still am.

ABOUT THE AUTHOR

I've worked in most all aspects of horticulture – garden centers, wholesale greenhouses, as a landscape designer, and finally as city horticulturist, where I took care of 20+ gardens around the city. I live in northwest Missouri with my husband and kids, the best little family that ever walked the earth. In 2012, when I was hugely pregnant, I graduated from Hamline University with a master's of writing for children; three weeks later, I had a son. It was quite a time.

My first book, **Courageous Women of the Civil War: Soldiers, Spies, Medics, and More** was published by Chicago Review Press in August 2016. This is a series of profiles of women who fought or cared for the wounded during the Civil War.

I've been sending novels out to publishers and agents since 1995, and have racked up I don't know how many hundreds of rejections. I kept getting very close — but not close enough. Agents kept saying, "You're a very good writer, you have an excellent grasp of craft, but I just don't feel that 'spark'...." Even after *Courageous Women* was published, they still weren't interested in my books.

In September 2016, I rage-quit traditional publishing and started self-publishing, because I wanted to get my books out to people who *would* feel that 'spark.' In my first year, I published 15 books. This year I plan to repeat that. (When you've been writing novels for over 20 years, you're going to have a bit of a backlog.) I am working my way completely through it and having a complete blast. I love doing cover work and designing the book interiors. I work full-time as a proofreader, so I handle that in my books as well.

And now I'm finding fans of my books who do feel that 'spark.' They're peaches, every one of them.

I'm finally doing what I was put on this earth to do.

There's no better feeling than that.

If you like this book, please leave a review on my Amazon or Goodreads page. Reviews help me get more readers.

Thanks so much for reading!
melindacordell.com

Subscribe to my newsletter
and get a free gardening book:
https://www.subscribepage.com/garden

CPSIA information can be obtained
at www.ICGtesting.com
Printed in the USA
LVHW011739160921
697990LV00010B/533